Grateful acknowledgement is made to the following pub
lications in which some of these poems first appeared: *Lak*
Street Review and *Sing Heavenly Muse!*

ISBN 0-935697-00-4
Library of Congress Catalog Card Number: 85-62685

First Edition

First Printing — Fall, 1985

Design by Tom Egerman
Photo by Ann Marsden
Typesetting by Red Sky Typesetting & Graphics

PAYMENTS DUE

PAYMENTS DUE

by Carol Connolly

Midwest Villages and Voices Publications
3220 10th Avenue South
Minneapolis, Minnesota 55407

CONTENTS

IV

V

FROM MIDWEST VILLAGES AND VOICES

Midwest Villages and Voices was founded to form a network to claim our culture. Art enhances our senses — whether in the form of words, visions, sound or movement.

How we live is our culture. Everything one does, thinks, hears, touches or sees is a part of one's culture. Each person's life reflects the many forms of art and communication which that person has experienced.

Midwest Villages and Voices understands that there are as many artists and artisans in our community as there are people. We also understand that most people do not perceive themselves as artists or they believe that culture is something in the distance, out of reach.

Payments Due reveals Carol Connolly's world of experience — all that glitters and all that hurts and all that astounds. The play on words, the biting insights on aging and change, the pathos of her verse: not pretty, but beautiful, profound, exposing. The many roles she's explored have not held her captive — mother, politician, poet, wife, single woman, activist, feminist — instead she has developed as woman, speaking her truth, pure, whole, sad and bright, the light of uncovering.

This book is a celebration of a woman and her poetry.

Let the Voice of the People Be Heard!

I.

ROMANCE

In every romance
there is a time, early,
when I want to consume him,
own him,
lock him in a closet in my vicinity.
A closet with a window.
I am not a killer.
I want to put him in a box,
carry him with me,
and if he, without looking,
steps into the box,
I close the cover quickly,
bang it shut,
and hang it with a heavy padlock.

As I turn the key in the lock,
I look at him curled in the box,
and think
"You idiot. What are you doing in that box?"

ON THE CONFINES OF MARRIAGE

"Save 20% on our collection of
Legant Diamonds!"
the advertisers command
in typographical error.
They will have to find an e.
Will they take it from
he or from she.
The e.
Whose pronoun will it deplete?

A SMALL PLUG FOR BIG COOLING

Not humidity. Heat.
Some vegetable gardens are in trouble.
Soft rotted bottoms,
male flowers drop off.
There are not enough bees around
and vine borers spread the disease.
Make notes.
Consider an insecticide.

A return of normal
growing weather
should set things right.

THE AFFAIR

When we met we knew.
When we met anew
We knew we knew.
Then I brought my children
And you were drunk.
Dead ends do end in
Dead ends.

TARNISH

Her flesh hot from a morning
on the desert,
she steps over the stone hedge
of sharp words and silence
piled between them
in the days just past.
He opens his arms to her.
She clings to him,
whispers of her want,
begs for the comfort
of his body,
and he says,
"As soon as I have my toast."

He wonders aloud as he chews,
tiny dry crumbs trembling on his lower lip,
he wonders
why spoons tarnish
and jam furrs.

SIXTH STREET

The clouds are blown off.
We sit here on the dark side of the house.
The truth stands silent between us,
at attention,
heels of its worn shoes pressed together.

In fighting everydayness
I sought a Sunday sort of man.
Oh, how the sun shone from him.
Today, the rain persists.
Through the transom I see

five chimneys atop five rowhouses
that rise through the wet lilacs.
the clock shows five oh five.
People who pull the petals from daisies
should part at an uneven hour.

The door that swings both ways
opens and closes tight.
You say goodby at six oh six.
I have been in this cave before,
fingered every inch.

I know it is the same garden
before and after the storm
and a wildflower that appears to be
finished
renews itself without invitation.

WHAT IF

A woman with thick ankles knows early that she
    has no power.

What if a pebble hits my windshield and continues on
    through my left eye, or
what if you write a hit song and leave me for a blond
    girl with slender legs, tan like bamboo, or
write a hit play and leave me for a blond
    boy with slender legs, tan like bamboo, or
what if your oil well gushes and you leave me
    for a cowgirl.

What if you leave and never return,
    and worse, what if you return and never leave.
I fear being alone, but what if I tell you that
    even more I fear never being alone.
You say your vows are true. You hold me,
    murmur low, promise me the stars,
but where will you be tomorrow?
    What if I can't find a place to park?

REGRETS

Wanting you,
not wanting you,
in dread of you
I tell myself once more
that dozens of daisies
and boxcars of berries
and moonsongs
and marathon dancing
and love given blind with passion
do not make regrets.

Regrets are made of nothing,
blank spaces and empty places
are mummy cases for a beating heart.
Things undone are bricks
layered on things unsaid,
the dare not taken
the hand not held
the gaze not met
eyes kept dry,
all mortared with quiet
and finished
with code words
prescribed by Emily Post.

DIVORCED

I am alone, single, solitary,
separated, celibate.
I have borne eight children.
I worry now
that I will die
a virgin.

II.

YOU WERE SOMETHING MORE THAN
YOUNG AND SWEET AND FAIR

for Lee Norman

She is my mother,
my daughter,
my sister.
She is a new woman,
an old woman,
a wise woman.
she is a legator of
faith and hope and generosity.
she puts her hand to strong things,
and she is clothed with strength and dignity.
she laughed at the days to come.
She is all of us,
and part of her is none of us
for she is one in her talent
and her wisdom and her gift for giving.
We call her friend,
and the sun, with its face shining,
remembers her.

FAST SHADOWS

She is seated in ceremony,
taps her fingers on the table
casting fast shadows
on the cafe's linen cloth,
every fiber stretched white.
She slowly crosses her legs.
Never will they know again
the weight of her husband's body.
He abandoned her without notice.
Gave in to a failing heart
on a tennis court in Mexico.
They were there to outwit
the white of winter.
Now, once more,
she uncrosses her long white widow's legs
and feels the weight
of the quiet loneliness of solitude,
waits for the arrival
of a new man she knows but little.
Stares.
Contemplates cockroaches
and dreads their fast shadows,
the way they appear and disappear
in silence
without notice.

THE EMPTY DRAWER

Its yellow eye stares at you.
An empty drawer left open,
a room stripped,
waiting for the painter.
A porch light burning after midnight.
It stares at you from a dark house.

It hums. A train in the distance
moving slowly. You watch it,
a train going South without you.
It hums in women's voices
from a television, unwatched
in the next room.
Hums from a telephone
that rings a wrong number.
Hums and whines,
a mosquito on a quiet night.

It sits next to you
in an empty theatre seat.
Its cold hands bind your arms to your sides.
It stalks about a crowded room,
follows you, turns laughing voices
into an icy waterfall.

You say softly and simply in sadness,
"I am lonely".
He says as he smiles, smokes a cigarette,
shuffles the pages of yesterday's news,
swaggers with his baggage,
he says
"It's bad taste to take anything too seriously."

TURKEY

He is a man
more ordinary
than he thinks.
As a child
he ate Wheaties
at Thanksgiving.
Everyone else ate
turkey.
He thought
he might not like
turkey.

LONG SHADOWS

My children walk back and forth under the moon.
Their long shadows criss-cross in quick x's
and loom before them.
They carry oranges through the snow
and brown sacks of milk and eggs
with no thought to the space not filled,
the long dark empty space before them.

My children. Prepare yourselves.
Say thank you and wipe your feet.
that sweater is too warm.
Don't spill the milk.
Careful with the eggs.
Lower your voices
and watch out for the long shadows.

TWO BABIES

I had two babies,
if you count twins as two.
I asked for a warm robe,
something sturdy
to wrap out the chill of two a.m.
He gave me yards of pink marabou.
He wanted me to be a naive girl
whose dancing would make
the fragile feathers float
up and down,
I wanted the insult
of his foolish feathers
plucked flat
so that no baby would be tickled
except by me.
I wanted him to understand.
Baby care is serious work.

He was a fool,
and so was I.

IMMACULATE CORRIDOR

In the locked ward,
from behind a door shut tight,
halting Chopin falls carefully
to the floor
one perfect chord
ahead of chaos.
Notice: Music Room
Locked
Midnight to 8:00 A.M.
Scant strength at sunrise
for a sleepless player
without a note
to call his own.
A burn like that
affects your whole system.

WELCOME

You understand that nothing ends.

A piper plays an Irish tune,
you hear its winter wail for days.
Someone promised
to be your friend for life.
You bury him.
The Priest in one breath
without comma without pause
chants and begs mercy
for those who know Death
or loss of love.

On a bright green day
you step through a new door.
A lady says in greeting
"I want to warn you.
Your husband is here.
With another woman."
You blink.
He divorced you.
The judge said it was final
three years ago.

III.

DOLLARS AND CENTS

Money is the color of mold.
Use it for a poultice
and it will infect your wound.
And you, you are
bad if you have it,
bad if you don't,
bad if you try to get it,
bad if you refuse,
bad if you lend it,
bad if you borrow it,
bad if you win it,
bad if you lose it,
foolish if you inherit it,
suspect if you ignore it.

Its fungus creeps
into the corners of marriages,
suffocates sons and daughters.
If you marry for money,
you will earn it.

SHALLOWS

for the 577 Demonstrators at Honeywell
Arrested on April 18, 1983

I want to float in the shallow water
close to the shore
where the sea is still,
the sand is white.

I want to loll
on my back on a puffed up life raft,
search for the silver lining,
gaze at the sky as blue as blue

glide straight into the sun,
and be consoled.
Never look back.
I have been in deep water.

I could
tell you stories
you would not
believe.

I will be alone now,
solitary, celibate.
I don't want to hear even a whisper
of the syllables in nuclear

the hiss in holocaust
the murder in mutilation.
I don't want to smell the sweat
in demonstrate or lobby or elect.

The kingfishers will roar by
in speedboats.
I won't even wave.
Far in the distance

the heat shimmers.
You may decide
to board a big boat,
chain your body to a war machine.

Remove all sharp objects
from your pockets
so you won't hurt yourself
or wound the cop who arrests you.

the steel door will bang behind you,
the jailor will say your time begins.
Keep in mind,
what is legal is not,

and as you pour your strength
into the deep ocean
that floats my raft close to the shore,
I will be safe in the sun

because you
hold back the dark
with your bare hands.

LAST RESORT

I am trapped here in a second rate body.
I. Me with the proper address,
and acceptable blood lines
and the appearance of a decent bank balance.
Trapped here at the pool
during the thigh show.
Sins of the flesh
are punished here. Exposed.
Sagging tits and a stretched belly
negate a person at this spa.
Here the only interest is in bones
and sinew and teeth and tan.
No flesh need apply.

Attention. Over here. I would
like to say that I am terribly sorry
if I have visually assaulted you.
I want to explain. I followed the rules.
It was seven pregnancies for me
and twins and nine pound babies.

Do you know that
if you want to have your cake,
you must eat it.

LADY POET AT LUNCH

At a small table of big time poets,
leaning into their strong winds,
she politely waves the clean vowels,
polished consonants of her smallest poems.
Unheard.
Contemplates a table knife through a heart,
a fork plunged into an open hand,
knows the Irishman would see
the beginnings of a stigmata,
wishes instead for paper pompoms
to act the proper
cheerleader.
Pompoms
to whish rah rah
as expected, and yet maintain
the required silence.
Rah rah.
Silent sis boom bah.

Afterwards, safe in her kitchen,
she waits
for her new skin to thicken,
says time spent with the big time
may be time misspent,
feels invisible,
and her son says "Invisible?
But you look nice."

DILLETTANTE

I am a full-time fraud,
passing as a poet.
It's filthy work. But,
someone has to do it.
Stilted syllables
line my walls,
confusion
crowds my room
with maggotty mounds
of mediocre metaphors,
ridicule lurks
in my hallway,
ambitious people
take all the best lines,
and I have a headache.
I woke up with it. But,
everyone wakes up
with something.

THE KEY

Some of you are winners.
Some of you are losers.
You know who you are.
If you become trapped
in this elevator,
do not
become excited.
Use the phone.
Call security.
The guard will
put a key in his ear
and wax will lubricate
the mechanism.
A lot of people
are having trouble
with their ears
these days.

NTOZAKE SHANGE VISITS MINNESOTA

Life is limitations. Woman, brilliant, exotic woman reads her poems full of color and wild movement, says she began to read in saloons when she was 19. At 19, I was looking for a career to marry, reading Amy Vanderbilt and Emily Post, and knew nothing of poetry. I blame the nuns. They never mentioned poems. All the best poets are divorced. Exotic woman embraces her culture, sees its flaws and celebrates. If her elders told her to cross her legs and bind her breasts, she paid no attention. She smokes Kools, in a chain, chants of love and rape, of freedom, commandos in brown boots, abstracts time in countries I can't spell. I watch this woman stomp out golden words and silver, I know that life is limitations and I don't like it. I slip into wishing I had a Milky Way to bite, its wrapper stamped "satisfaction guaranteed," fill my mouth with its sweet soft brown mass, fill it, and leave no room in my head for the knowledge that life is limitations.

MY SISTERS

On the Tenth Anniversary
of the Creation of the
DFL Feminist Caucus

When madness descends,
wraps itself around my legs,
begins to paralyze me,
You, My sisters, hold me
on this side of the fine line
that divides sunlight
from insanity.
You are the warmth of spring
to my frozen field,
the summer rain
to my drought,
You are the moon
in my midnight.
Your steadfast wisdom
surrounds me
in circles that ripple out
and hold my daughters
and their daughters
in a place where
the sun shines brightest
and strength
blooms.
Awesome in its beauty.

LIZZY BORDEN

Lizzy Borden took an ax
gave her mother forty whacks,
when she saw what she had done,
gave her father forty-one.

I understand you, Lizzy Borden.
You end it, forty whacks
with a cleaver or an ax,
say no to the vows,
give the contract a decent burial,
plant white flowers,
move on,
check your bags
with any handy porter,
and still
a long first marriage stays with you
a mark on your soul
like mother's words
and father's warnings
wanting Extreme Unction.

You see the reflection of your own face
in a cloudy mirror that won't come clean.

NO LOLLING

No lolling around.
No lolling around in bed.
No lolling on sofas. Or overstuffed chairs.
It was my mother's foremost rule.
I was an energetic loller.
An expert at lolling in and on.
When lounging pajamas came into fashion,
I recognized their acceptable chic.
I never was successful at lounging.
Even now, I remain
devoted to sprawled lolling.
Keep in practice.
But I will admit,
since my mother is gone,
I loll
with less verve.

AN ORDINARY EVENT

The fact that it happens
to all of us
doesn't make it any easier.

I turned a corner
and suddenly
without warning
I stand full
before a mirror,
and there it is.
My mother's face
staring back at me
in disbelief.
The face
I swore
I'd never have.

MIRROR, MIRROR

The morning news is brought to you by
the national association for stutterers,
umbrellas bloom like violets on 57th street,
at the coffee shop, forty-two chickens turn
on seven spits, sputter in the heat.
He announces that I must improve. Firm
up. Consider a face lift. He tells me he
has seen women become man's best
friend after a lift. O.K.
I consider it. I learn to spell
Ponce de Leon, and for a while,
I never pass a mirror without stopping
to push at my forehead, my eyes,
pull at my throat, stare
at the possibilities of youth,
confront myself from every sagging side,
and in the end, I know. The best
way to improve is to
stand alone. Take time
to practice my pirouette as I
turn to embrace age
with the same gusto
I squandered youth.

IV.

MAN'S BEST FRIEND

In the Center
of the Empire
men dress in fine ensembles
and walk the dog.
They bend beneath curbs,
gather warm dog excrement
in clear bags pulled
from fine silk pockets.
Only the finest.
This is the Center
of the Empire,
where money talks
and dogs are walked
on Gucci leashes
and dog dirt
is collected.
E is for Empire
its excellence
is elegant
but excrement
exists.
In piles.

NO VACANCY

Riding all night
past neon signs that blink
no vacancy.
Closed. No eggs for travelers.
Meeting dawn in a mountain town.
In small houses
close to the road
daily rituals are observed.
Coffee is cooking,
women crack eggs,
men shave in silence,
children stretch and yawn
on the edge of rumpled beds.
I am on the road.
Before the sun brings noon
I'll stretch my legs
in New York City.
Tomorrow is as fragile
as a sheer curtain pulled tight.
Any old dog
who comes along
can put his paw
through it.

CAREFREE ARIZONA

In a garden pruned, meticulous,
patrolled each day at dawn,
grass kept green in desert heat,
an unfeathered bird intrudes,
prostrate and still
on my threshold
in the Sun of Sunday noon.
Translucent skin spreads from its
tiny baby body, wings
outstretched in silent salute
to a parade
of insects moving in
to stand attention.
Born at sunrise,
dead before noon,
its courage will
never
stand the test
of the chill
that comes in the dark
just before dawn.

FRIDAY NIGHT FLIGHT

The desert sky at dusk
is painted with a broad brush.
We bend beneath an arch of oleander
emerge into the confetti
of new stars. Turning
from bells of laughter
we climb on the Friday night flight
for Purgatory.
This began in innocence,

a planned assault on continuity,
a stop in Jerome where fragile
houses grip the mountainside
on slender stilts. Geronimo
was a teamster here, and then
he was immortalized.
Safeway declares in weathered perpetuity
its pledge to distribution
without waste.

I did not surrender
to his pink shirt.
I was not swayed by his eyes
blue as the desert sky,
by the majesty of red rocks
in the sun of Sedona,
by mountain air sweet
in a field of yellow flowers.
It happened during the night.

He took my hands in his firm grip
and kissed my fingers
in his sleep.

BAGGAGE

There are some things you have to expect.
If you ride on airplanes,
sooner or later,
you stand by that great roulette wheel
that spits out baggage
and your number will not come up.
You look back in fondness at past luck
when misgivings were temporary,
and accept the empty chute.
You don't have a grip.

You are stranded
in New York without a nuance
to call your own.
There may be abuses.
Your well-kept secrets
have escaped into space
and your permanent point of view
is loose with your toothbrush
wrapping itself in your reputation.

Reality is something you rise above,
but the longing
to drag your baggage
lingers.

SIDE TRIP FROM SOUTHHAMPTON

The sun blazes
and there is no shelter
on Shelter Island
where the deepest blue
hydrangeas, wild in their profusion,
are full blown,
just this side of rot.

In the harbor
the air is still.
Sails down, boats
are stacked
like cordwood
in this unrelenting heat.

He promises
to light my cigarettes
with dollar bills.
I don't smoke.
And the marigolds.
A piercing, blinding yellow,
more yellow
and bigger
than I ever remember.

SURRENDER TO HENRI BENDEL

In white rooms
filled with the white notes
of heavy metal
everyone wears white
with their tan.
A tiny dark woman,
her face intricately scarred,
takes my hand and leads me
to water.
This is a beauty shop.
She speaks only Iranian, Darling,
her assistant speaks only Chinese, Darling,
and their idea of beauty
and mine
may not be the same.
There is no way of knowing.

THEY SAY IT'S A CLICHE´

One day at dawn you open a window
    on a new city and see
that not much is right
    and in your neighborhood
not much is wrong,
    that some rights are not granted,
and some wrongs cannot be righted,
    that money is king,
and beauty is queen,
    and romance rescues only the naive.
You wrap your arms around the truth
    that you are
        a middle-aged
        middle class
        middle weight contender
        for a mid-life crisis.

V.

IN A WORD

A woman I met
briefly
and only
by chance,
said
"I like your
boyfriend,
but you are
smarter
than he is."
It had never
occurred to me.
I thought
it over.
He is taller,
stronger,
prettier,
younger,
and she's right.
I am
smarter.
This news
changes
everything.

PAYMENTS DUE

Armed with
a full list
of infallible rules,
I was finished
in a convent school
where ladies
do not speak
of dollars or cents.
I ambled on
to other exclusive shelters,
white linen, white flowers,
and shade.
In the end
it all exploded.
And I was born.
Late.
Yelling and struggling
into the real world
of debits and credits,
bid and ask,
payments due
or else.

You. My Hero.
Tall, suave and smug.
You stepped in
to fill the hole
in my heart.
You flex your muscles
within my womb,
hold your breath
just above water.
Neglect your mortgage
and fold at foreclosure.
Your dry feet
do not touch ground.
Smoke from your flame
grows dangerously dense.
My rules said
you would take care of
me.

A GENTLEMAN'S INVITATION

Meet me at six o'clock
at the New French Cafe.
We will share,
says he,
a cup of consomme.
Handsome is he
and debonnaire.
His smile is as wide
as the English Channel.
But a hungry woman
searching for substance
could
drown
in a cup of consomme
at six o'clock
at the New French Cafe.

ODE TO A MESSAGE

She answered the telephone,
said, "yes, yes,"
and drew a grecian urn
on the message pad.
The rim of its perfect neck
flush with the paper's edge
as though to say "No
to any wildflowers in my urn.
No to any spilling of my wine."

Into the telephone
she hummed "of course, yes, yes,"
as she drew a second urn
and then a third,
all in the same position.

REJECTION

No thanks for your work
the editor says.
This requires
two typewritten pages.
Cut your poems up,
he says.
Line by line.
Put the lines together in a hat.
Pull them out.
One at a time.
And see what happens.

Ah. But
I don't
have a hat.

MAILMAN

I waited each day, through
an hour locked in yellow light,
stood at attention
and watched for the clock to read 10:00.
Around 10:00 the mailman rings the bell.
I hoped with excruciating intensity,
fingers tightly crossed,
for some word from you,
some small curl from your pen.
Now you are with me.

This morning, I watch you.
You annoy me.
You came here to ruin 10 o'clock.
You make the mail nothing.

IS THIS A JOKE

He invited a student to live in their house,
to work in exchange for lodging.
He began to take brandy to bed,
to cover the glass with a paperback book
to save it from evaporation during the night.
His wife woke him,
shook his shoulder. She asked,
"Do you love the student more than me?"
He resisted, feigned sleep,
rustled the sheets, groaned,
and finally resigned himself
to a true/false answer.
"Yes."
His wife announced
she would now kill herself.
Put her head in their oven.
As she turned from their marriage bed,
her elbow tipped the brandy.
It bled into the pages of his soft book.

After some blank time,
with nothing to read or drink,
he ventured to their kitchen.
Curious, he wondered if she knew:
to suicide,
you must blow out the pilot light.
"How is it going?"
His wife, her golden hair dull
with carbon and sweat
said "It's hot in here."

DIARY

He shakes his finger
and wails
that I have
written long passages
in his private diary.
I say, I'm sorry.
I didn't think.
And don't you worry.
I wrote in pencil.
I don't admit
that I pressed
as hard as I could
on his fine white paper
near the back
where the pages were blank,
close to the blood red cover.
No amount of erasing
will take me out of his book.

DEAR JOHN

I don't want to think about this
but sometimes
a memory seeps like steam through
the frozen glass of my pond.

I stood once at the ancient sink
that hangs steadfast on my kitchen wall,
its innards exposed,
held the hand of Brigid

our seventh born,
stared at the rope of garlic
hung to ward off vampires,
and you said I was a parasite.

Parasite, you said.
Who knows when anything ends.

I see you everywhere these days,
in crowds and couples.
Never is it you. Not once.
I dream you wear a beard.

Brigid says it's true. You do.
And your new sink grinds garbage.
This pale new woman, quiet.
she smokes so many cigarettes.

You call her fiance.
Is she a virgin?
I want to know.

BELOW ZERO

Dangerous weather.
Windchill 65⁰ below zero.
I tell you I have seen, just now,
on the freeway leading from Minneapolis,
thirteen cars stalled,
five cars in one wreck,
and a sports car descending,
taillights in a spiral,
over the edge of a bridge.

You say "my god,"
the whine of ridicule in your voice,
"Life and death within a mile.
A veritable working girl's Vietnam."
as though the only
valid experience
this weather is yours.

Do I still love you?
It's like riding a bicycle.
If I begin again
I'll be able to do it.

BLUE COVERS

My third son,
the charming one,
the toker,
dope smoker,
keeps his reefer paper
with his lunch tickets
between the blue covers
of his algebra text,
blue as his eyes,
as blue as the Irish river
that runs through my soul.
No grades in algebra for him.
His brains are going up in smoke.

I have wrung my hands
through car wrecks,
stolen checks,
failing grades,
and promises made
then broken.
He comes to
just long enough
to blubber
that he has lost my trust.

Yes.
And he is about
to lose my interest.

CELEBRATION

I hear news
of a 37th wedding anniversary
and think,
my god.
It would be nice.
In case either party
requires any sort of amputation,
there will be
no need
for anesthetic.

CALCULATOR

I know
my numbers
are all wrong.
They divide into
too many years,
an uneven number
of children,
months in cities
where only
local time is observed
and white flowers wilt,
weeks of existing conditions,
absurdities, imprecisions,
days and days and days
misspent,
and you.
You brought me
a string of pearls.
Pearls are nice,
but a woman
with high numbers
should have
a string of zeros.
Six or seven
shiny ciphers
hanging
from a simple digit
for comfort
in the dark days
of November
when the nights
are long.

TIGHTROPE

You walk a tightrope alone.
No one can help you.
Anyone who holds your hand
might be out for murder.

If a tall mysterious acrobat,
just the right wave in his dark hair
comes to you gathering silence
like a marathon runner,
says he can tame lions,
make molehills out of monsters,
curl your hair, cure your nightmares,
says he owns a net,
says his net is new,
you might chance touching his fingers.

If you put your hand in his,
oh! it is warm and strong!
you could lose your balance.
You must walk a tightrope alone.

OLD QUESTIONS

There is a piano here in this new place,
this place that promised new answers to
old questions.
A slim ebony upright piano in the foyer
stands in the shadows gathering city dust.
Steadfast in its stillness, it waits,
calling out in long dark silent oh's
for a piano player.
There are few words
from you, here in this new place.

If you were here, in this new place,
your sharp and flat notes would
fall all over the rooms here,
wrinkle the smooth sheets,
cover the floors with confetti,
blow out the windows,
bend the trees in Riverside Park,
and splash into the Hudson River.

The Coast Guard would knock hard at this door,
people in this building would ring me with complaints
and the bone-thin woman who holds a mute dog,
her eyes dart about the elevator in search of order,
would have me evicted here,
from this new place.

IT'S NOT GOING WELL

Five years
of one man's adoration
and undying devotion
is enough for anyone.
When I told him I
wanted to separate,
he leapt like someone
shot.
Now the whole house
smells of wounded buffalo.
And he continues
to serve tea
in the best china
exactly
at midnight.

ICE BOX

His silence separates us,
a sheet of blue ice.
It reflects the light
of my devotion,
dim as a 15 watt bulb.
He floods the ice
and sweeps it with secrets
locked like lasers in his eyes.

The oxygen level is low
in this ice box.
No heavy breathing allowed.
No rage. No fury.
No hammering of aching hearts.
No splashing of hot tears.

Keep it still.
If the ice cracks
and begins to melt,
we will rot like chickens
freezer burned since Christmas.

AUGUST

It is a shipboard romance
on land as dry as brown pastures,
fifteen day sail through
intemperate zones,
blue rooms, sweet songs,
your green eyes agate hard
with pain not yet abandoned
and a single tear is trapped
in the stem of your crystal glass
as the catatonia of hard desire
plays out on silent saxaphones.

The horizon is bright with a new sun,
we make shadows on a tin bird
and swing on dark porches.
I know there is music in night life,
Stoddard will lecture
in brave words, not foolish,
that Mars remains,
the world will never end,
and I wonder
if you make outgoing calls
from your sensible black telephone.

EVEN-NUMBERED YEARS

This nightmare recurs
more often
in even-numbered years.
You bring words set to music,
white flowers,
dance before me,
tell me you worship
the curve of my hip,
the touch of my cool white hand.
I run in place,
whistle to scramble your sounds,
wipe the sweat from my palms,
stop at last
for air
and your music takes over.
Slowly I bend to you
lock my eyes into yours,
and you methodically
using the principles of logic
and philosophy,
prove to me
I am an asshole.
Prove I indulge myself
in a piercing lack of integrity,
and strange beliefs
about the right to happiness.

Watch me now.
I will indulge myself,
love/hate you with a volcanic rage,
hotter than your mouth,
prop up what little integrity
I keep buried with the bones of birds,
and warn you. Never come to me again.
Your white flowers have wilted.
They always do.

IT WAS A VERY MAD AFFAIR

There was music between us,
the joy of
clean sweet jazz.
Then you began to beat
your drum in solo.
Hard and fast
you beat it
to a vicious decible.
The veins in your neck
stood out
blue, like twilight.
I had to cover my ears
and then my eyes.
At last,
even you admit it.
You can't take the noise.

I sink slowly,
best foot first
into serene solitude.
And still,
somedays I wonder.
Can I take the silence?

OSTRICH EGG

She kept her life in an egg shell,
tended it carefully.
A pale blue shell,
ornate with gold leaf.
Safe, she thought,
in her airtight oval.

On a June night,
he thrust out a leg.
Deep in sleep,
he flung his leg across her,
cracked her shell beyond repair.
Some said righteously
He was violent.

She began to sleep alone,
emerging slowly
as the rupture
in her tended shell
grew wider.
She was last seen
smiling in a broad new way,
her lungs expanding
like sails full of strong winds.

THE INDEX

If you shake your finger at me again,
I will bite it off and hold the tip
in my teeth until I die.
People with
police power
will find it.
Trace you.
You will be
arrested.
In Duluth.

FANTASY

If my breasts were
as sharp and pointed
as the pyramids,
I would use them
to cut
red x's
in your face.

Carol Connolly, when she was 40, wanted to learn to write fiction, but the class was closed. She entered a poetry workshop instead and she has been writing poetry ever since. Born, raised, and educated in the Irish Catholic section of Saint Paul, Minnesota, she has seven children, five of whom were born within four years. Connolly has worked to change the status of women. She has diligently helped to secure the appointment and election of women to positions in every level of government. Connolly served as Chair of the Minnesota Women's Political Caucus, served for nine years on the St. Paul Human Rights Commission, acting as Chair for three years, and is presently a member of the Minnesota Racing Commission, chairing the Affirmative Action Committee of that Commission. Carol Connolly lives in St. Paul with her youngest daughter, Brigid, and for part of each year, works in New York City for a foundation that gives awards to women over 40. She has read her poems around the country. This is her first book.

MIDWEST VILLAGES AND VOICES
Minneapolis, Minnesota 1985

Also available from Midwest Villages and Voices:

Rites of Ancient Ripening, by Meridel Le Sueur (published by the author), $5.00. Collection of poetry.

Every Woman Has a Story, edited by Gayla Wadnizak Ellis (published by the editor), $8.00. A collection of writings, songs and visual art about Midwestern life, compiled from contributions from 50 women.

America: Song We Sang Without Knowing, by Neala Schleuning (published by Little Red Hen Press), $8.00. The life and ideas of Meridel Le Sueur.

People, Pride and Politics: Building the North Star Country, by Pandora Productions, Minneapolis, MN, $15.00/individuals, $100.00/institutions. Six one-half hour shows from a radio series (three cassette tapes).

Worker Writer, by Meridel Le Sueur (published by West End Press), $2.00. Revised from 1939 pamphlet for the Minnesota Writers Project of Works Progress Administration.

Keystone for Survival, by Black Hills Alliance, $4.00. Findings and reports from presentations at Citizens Review Commissions on Energy-Developing Corporations at Black Hills International Survival Gathering held outside Rapid City, S.D., in 1980.

Hard Country, by Sharon Doubiago (published by West End Press), $ 8.00. Poetry.

Crusaders, by Meridel Le Sueur (published by Minnesota Historical Society Press), $5.00. A biography about her parents, Marion and Arthur Le Sueur.

I Hear Men Talking, by Meridel Le Sueur (published by West End Press), $5.95. A collection of short stories.

We also have some works-in-progress. Please write for more information. To place orders, add $1.00 postage for first book, 50¢ each additional; Minnesota residents add 6% sales tax. MV & V, 3220 - 10th Avenue South, Minneapolis, MN 55407 (mail order only).